HOW TO MAKE SALSA

© 2001 by Barbara Soden

All rights reserved. No part of this book may be reproduced or transmitted in any form or by any means, electronic or mechanical, including photocopying, recording or by any informational storage or retrieval system, except by a reviewer who may quote brief passages in a review to be printed in a magazine or newspaper-without permission in writing from the publisher.

This book is for all the people who love salsa now and for those who, hopefully, will learn to love it after trying these recipes.

And to my friend, Cheryl Chapman, for her very creative drawings and to everyone else who were so generous with their favorite recipes.

Enjoy!

TABLE OF CONTENTS

About Salsas	6-10
Salsa Tips	11-14
Chile Types	15-21
Other Ingredients Explained	22-26
Handling Chiles	27-33
Making a Ristra	34-38
Vegetable Salsas	39-111
Fruit & Dessert Salsas	112-157
Miscellaneous	158-171

ABOUT SALSAS

Moving to southern New Mexico 5 years ago from the Chicago area, not only brought a change in culture but also in the food we are learning to love.

The Las Cruces area is part of the "Chile Capital of the World". Chiles grow in abundance here and the fields in the late summer are filled with people picking the chiles for market. You can go into the local supermarket and buy bags of chiles and have them roasted while you wait. The smell is unbelievably wonderful and you know fall is on the way.

In early fall the chiles that are left on the vine turn a bright red and are harvested and dried and marketed or made into ristras to use at a later date. They can be kept for extended periods as long as they are kept cool and dry then can be rehydrated and used in cooking.

Using chiles in recipes gives a whole new meaning to flavorful. They are a wonderful addition. So just enjoy!

The word "salsa", is Spanish for sauce. Salsa can be made with any vegetable or fruit combination of regional ingredients you may choose and does not have to be "hot". It's a staple of the southwestern United States and can be used, not only on chips and crackers, but as a condiment for beef, fish, chicken, or any kind of meat, or as a side dish. There are cooked and uncooked salsas but all are relatively easy to make

Fresh ingredients are best but are not always available, so canned or frozen ingredients can be substituted.

However when the summer harvest is in and the local markets or farm stands are abundant with fresh produce, purchase them then, they can be frozen for future use.

Chiles are especially great roasted, either by you or from the market. They can be stored in zip lock bags with skin and seeds intact and frozen. They can be used not only in salsas but as toppings for burgers, chile rellenos or anything your imagination can dream up.

When making these recipes feel free to substitute any

chiles that you choose. Each will create a different flavor. For a milder salsa, bell peppers can be used instead of the hotter varieties. Create your own flavors.

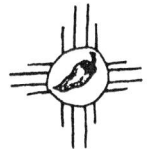

SALSA TIPS

- Use fresh ingredients whenever possible.

- Use a sharp knife for a clean cut for mincing and dicing.

- Experiment a lot. You will get a feel for salsas and the combinations of the right flavors and colors.

- Always taste before adding the hot spices. You can always add more.

- Salsas are made from high acid ingredients thus keep well in the refrigerator for about 1 week, some will keep longer.

- Store in glass or ceramic bowls or jars.

- When serving frozen salsa, defrost thoroughly and stir well before serving.

- Some of the recipes call for roasted tomatoes. This will give the tomatoes a different taste, more robust and flavorful. This can be done the same way as the chiles in a broiler or grill, but do not over blacken or they will acquire a bitter taste.

- Roasting the garlic will give it sweeter and more subtle flavor then fresh garlic.

- When choosing chiles, the wider the shoulder and the blunter the tip usually signifies a milder chile.

- As a rule, the smaller the chile the hotter it is.

- Chiles are hotter at the stem end than at the tip.

- Green chile pods are considered a vegetable. Red are considered a spice.

- Salsa is high in fiber and low in fat and calories, so therefore, the perfect food.

- Chiles are members of the Capsicum family, which also includes their milder cousins known as peppers.

- Bell peppers got their name because they are shaped like a bell.

CHILE TYPES

Ancho - Ripened and dried poblanos (sometimes called pasilla). Large and rounded, dark color, wrinkled skin. Mild but flavorful.

Arbol - Small dried red chiles, about 2-1/2" long and narrow. They are usually dried serrano peppers. These are very hot.

Banana or Hungarian Was -Fairly long with waxy yellow skins that turn red with age.

Bell Peppers - These peppers can be substituted for a hotter chile to cut the heat in recipes. The red are fully mature green bells and are very sweet and flavorful.

California Anaheim - A long green chile that is flavorful when roasted. These are mild but the seeds can be left in for a spicier taste.

Chipotles - Ripened, smoke dried Jalapeños. They are very hot but add a wonderful smoky flavor to foods.

Habañeros - A fiery chile also know as Scotch bonnet. It is extremely hot.

Jalapeños - The most popular chile in the United States. Can be eaten raw or roasted, but always remove the seeds.

New Mexico Red - These are said to be hotter than California chiles. These are usually sold on strings - "ristras".

Pequins - A tiny little red chile that packs a punch. They are nutty and flavorful and are very hot.

Serrano - A popular chile now found often in the U.S. It is light green and has a good heat to it.

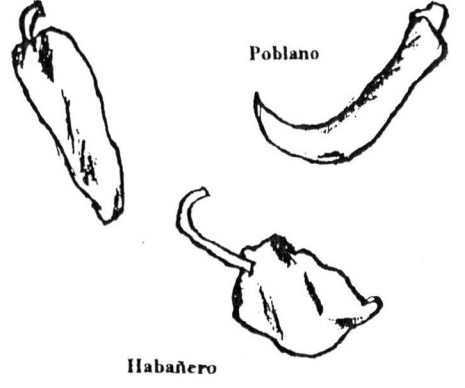

Anaheim
(or New Mexico Green)

Poblano

Habañero

Banana
(or Hungarian Wax)

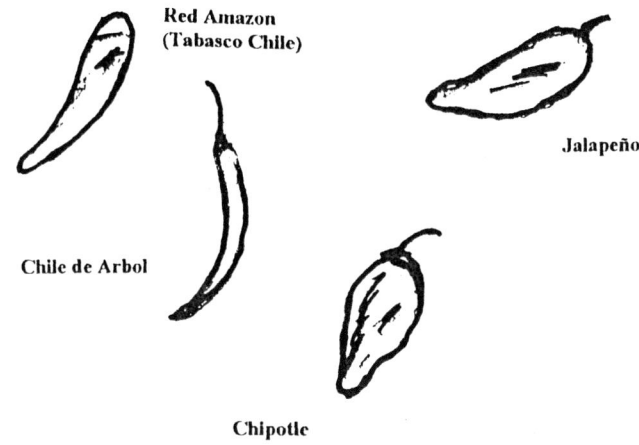

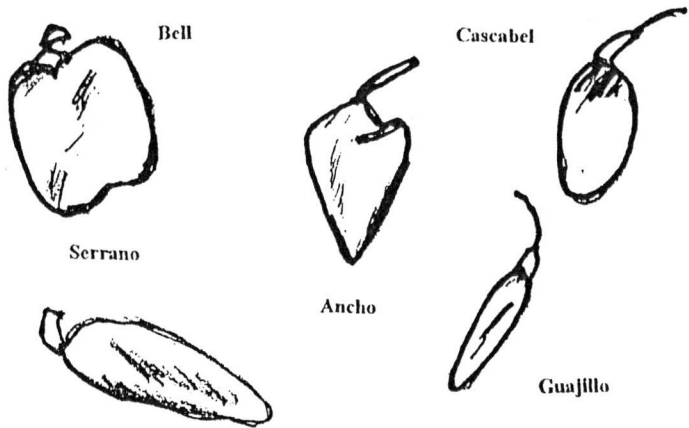

OTHER INGREDIENTS EXPLAINED

Avocados - A wonderful addition to any salsa. This creamy fruit is a counterpoint to the hot chiles. For best results when using in salsa or any other dish, combine all ingredients first then add avocado at the last minute. Lime juice will prevent discoloration.

Beans (Frijoles) - Beans are one of the most important ingredients of southwestern cooking. Among the varieties are:

Black Beans - A very dark purple bean.

Pinto Beans - The most common, these are native of the southwestern U.S. Pinto means painted.

White Beans - Known also as navy beans.

Calabasa - A Mexican squash. Can be substituted with zucchini.

Cheese - Queso

Chile Relleno - A chile filled with some type of stuffing,

Chorizo - A spicy sausage.

Cilantro - Also known as coriander or Chinese parsley. This is a wonderful spice that can be used in almost anything. The stems can be chopped and eaten too.

Maíz - Corn

Jicama - A potato-like vegetable used in salads.

Masa - Corn flour that has been treated and is used to make tortillas and tamales.

Piñons - A nut of the pine tree.

Quesadilla - A fried or grilled tortilla with a filling.

Sopapilla - A deep fried, puffy bread usually served as a dessert.

Tamale - Masa with a filling and wrapped in corn husks and steamed until cooked.

Tomatillos - A member of the gooseberry family, these have a papery outer husk whisk must be peeled off. There is a sticky residue that has to be washed off with hot water before using. These can be used cooked or raw and add a tart flavor to any dish.

Tomatoes - Many of us cannot find good tomatoes all year round so when in doubt use Roma or plum tomatoes. These are meaty varieties and are especially good roasted, bringing out their full flavor.

Tostada - Fried tortilla served flat and topped with a variety of mixtures.

HANDLING CHILES

WARNING: Because of the capsaicin in the chiles they can burn the skin and anything that you touch while working with them. Always wear rubber gloves when handling chiles and never touch your eyes or face while working with them. This is very important.

Bell peppers are probably the only exception to this rule as they are very mild.

Another thing to remember is to remove the seeds when

you are cleaning the chiles, especially the jalapeño peppers. These are small and can cause problems if ingested.

If seeds are left in the other peppers it adds to the heat as they soak up the capsaisin. A newcomer to the chile world should take caution in adding chiles to their recipes, add a little at a time as you can always add more as you go along.

                                                      (more)

Don't let these simple cautions ruin your enjoyment of chiles, they are fun and interesting vegetables and give so much flavor to food. It's just a note of caution until you get use to handling them.

Because chile skins are tough and fibrous, they have to be either roasted or boiled before using.

Roasting: Use your broiler or grill to roast. First pierce the peppers with a sharp knife to keep them from
(more)

bursting as they roast. Place directly on the grill or in a roasting pan in the broiler. Turn often to keep them from burning, you only want to char the skins.

When skin is darkened on the outside, place them in a plastic bag or bowl and cover with a towel to "sweat". This will make the skins come off easily. When cool, wearing rubber gloves, remove from bag or bowl and take off the stem, the skin should peel right off. Some remnants of skin may remain but that will add to the flavor. You can also do this under running water, but it loses some of the flavor doing it this way.

           (more)

Bell peppers can be roasted too. It gives them a more smoky, enticing flavor than when raw. All bell peppers can be roasted, but the red seem to be the best because of their sweetness. Roast them the same way you would any other pepper, being careful not to overcook.

Boiling: Jalapeños should be boiled before using. Put chiles in saucepan and boil for about 10 minutes. Cool before peeling and discard the water.

(more)

Bell and habañero peppers, because they have thinner skins, can be used without roasting but can be roasted if you desire.

Rehydrating Dried Red Chiles: Place on a cookie sheet and roast in a 250° oven for a minute or two with the door open. Put in a bowl and pour boiling water over them and let stand for 1/2 to 1 hour. Remove seeds and stems and blend with a little of the water, then strain to remove any excess residue. This can be used

(more)

(continued)
immediately or frozen for future use.

When you roast peppers, do a large batch and store in plastic bags in the freezer for future use. They are wonderful to pull out of the freezer in the middle of winter when the harvest is long gone.

MAKING
A
RISTRA

Ristras, when hung by
the front door, are believed
to ward off evil spirits.

1. Tie clusters of 3 chiles with light-weight string.

1.

2. Wrap string around stems twice, looping under then upward between 2 of the pods. Tighten string to secure stems.

3. Make a half hitch with string and place it over the stems and pull tight. Continue to cluster and tie pods in this fashion until the weight makes it hard to handle. Break the string and start again.

4. The clusters are now ready for braiding. Suspend twine from top of door, or rafter. Make a loop at the bottom of the twine. Tie 2 strings of clusters at the loop and braid with twine. Position the chiles to protrude from different directions.

4.

VEGETABLE SALSAS

VEGETABLE SALSAS

Aunt Lupe's Salsa	45-46
Avocado Salsa I	47
Avocado Salsa II	48
Tomatillo-Avocado Salsa	49
Barbecue Salsa	50
Basil Tomato Salsa	51
Black Bean Salsa	52
Chile Black Bean Salsa	53
Buckshot Salsa	54
Cheese Chile Salsa	55

Cherry Tomato Salsa	56
Cheryl's Fresh Salsa	57
Cheryl's Extra Special Queso	58
Chile Radish Salsa	59-60
Chilean Salsa	61
Colorful Salsa	62
Charred Corn & Chile Salsa	63-64
Festive Corn Salsa	65
Mexican Corn Salsa	66
Roasted Corn Salsa	67
Easy Salsa	68
Freezer Salsa	69

Frijole (Bean) Salsa	70
Garden Herb Salsa	71
Garlic Salsa	72
Green Chile Salsa	73
Hot Stuff Salsa	74
Italian Salsa	75
Meat Salsa	76
Jalapeño Salsa	77-78
Mushroom Bacon Salsa	79-80
Mushroom & Tomato Salsa	81-82
New Mexican Salsa	83
Olive Salsa	84

Black Olive Salsa	85
Black Olive & Chive Salsa	86
Ripe Olive & Charred Onion Salsa	87-88
Two Olive Salsa	89-90
Carrots & Black Olive Salsa	91
Pico de Gallo	92
Texas Pico de Gallo	93
Quick Salsa	94
Red's Salsa	95-96
Salsa Cruda	97-98
Salsa Cilantro	99
Salsa Picante	100

Salsa Verde	101
Salsa Vino	102
Summer Vegetable Salsa	103
Tequila Salsa	104
Thai Salsa	105
Tomatillo Salsa I	106
Tomatillo Salsa II	107-108
Tomatillo Tomato Salsa	109
Versatile Salsa	110
Yellow Salsa	111

AUNT LUPE'S SALSA

8 jalapeños
1 lg. onion, chopped
2 med. tomatoes, cored
    and chopped
1 tsp. garlic powder
salt to taste
2 qts. water
2 T. cilantro, chopped

Rinse jalapeños, cut in half and seed and place in a large pot. Add onion, tomatoes, garlic, salt and water. Bring to a boil over medium-high heat and cook for 20 minutes. When done, pour into a strainer to remove

(continued)
water then place in food processor or blender and puree. Serve warm or refrigerate until ready to use. Let the salsa come back to room temperature before serving.

This is very hot. To make a milder version, double or triple the tomatoes.

AVOCADO SALSA I

1/2 c. avocado, finely diced
1-1/2 c. tomatoes, peeled, seeded and chopped
1/2 c. red onion, finely diced
1/4 c. parsley, finely chopped
1/4 c. jalapeño, finely diced
1/4 green bell pepper, finely diced
1/8 tsp. sugar (optional)

Mix all ingredients in a non-aluminum bowl. Add sugar and salt to taste. Let salsa sit at room temperature at least 1 hour. Stir well before serving.

AVOCADO SALSA II

3 jalapeños, seeded and minced
2 cloves garlic
3 sprigs cilantro, chopped
1 T. vegetable oil
3 lg. ripe avocados
4 lg. ripe tomatoes
1 medium onion, chopped
Juice of 1 lemon or lime
salt and pepper to taste

Peel and chop avocados and dice tomatoes. Combine all ingredients and refrigerate. This is great on beef tacos.

TOMATILLO-AVOCADO SALSA

1/3 lb. tomatillos, husked rinsed and quartered	1 T. olive oil
1/4 lb. jalapeño chiles, seeded and halved	1 firm-ripe avocado, peeled and diced
2 cloves garlic	1/2 c. minced onion
1/2 c. fresh cilantro	2 T. lime juice
	salt to taste

In blender or food processor, combine tomatillos, chiles, garlic and cilantro until coarsely pureed. Pour into a bowl. Stir in olive oil, avocado and onion. Add lime juice and salt to taste.

BARBECUE SALSA

2 c. tomatoes, seeded and diced
1-1/2 T. garlic vinegar
1/2 c. diced green chiles
1/3 c. onions, diced
1 c. green peas, frozen
1/4 tsp. ground cumin
2 T. dried cilantro, crushed

Combine all ingredients. Peas may be added frozen, they will thaw in the salsa. Refrigerate overnight for best flavor. Serve as a side dish with barbecue.

BASIL TOMATO SALSA

1/4 c. balsamic vinegar
2 T. Dijon mustard
1 T. red wine vinegar
1 T. basil oil

2 c. tomato, seeded and diced
1 c. fresh basil, chopped
2 clove garlic, crushed

Combine vinegar, mustard, red wine vinegar and oil in a bowl, whisking until blended. Add remaining ingredients and stir gently. Refrigerate before serving.

BLACK BEAN SALSA

1 can (15 oz.) black beans, drained
1 T. olive oil
1/2 c. pimentos, diced
1/8 tsp. cumin
1/2 c. fresh cilantro, chopped
4 green onions, diced
1 T. lime juice

Mix all ingredients together and refrigerate until well chilled. This is good with chicken and pork.

CHILE BLACK BEAN SALSA

2 cans black beans, drained
1/4 c. red onion, diced
1 clove garlic, minced
2 T. chile powder
1/2 tsp. ground cumin
1/2 c. fresh cilantro, chopped
Juice of 3 fresh limes
1/2 c. each green, red and yellow bell seeded and diced
1 poblano, roasted (see pg. 29), seeded and diced

Rinse black beans and mix all ingredients, adding lime juice last. Refrigerate 1 hour. Top with sour cream

BUCKSHOT SALSA

12 jalapeños, boiled and seeded

1 c. tomatoes
1/2 tsp. garlic salt

Combine all ingredients in food processor or blender. Chill. HOT, HOT, HOT!

CHEESE CHILE SALSA

1 pt. dry cottage cheese
1/2 c. mayonnaise
1 c. jalapeños. seeded and diced
1/3 c. red onion, diced
1 med. tomato, chopped
1 T. hot sauce

Put all ingredients in blender and blend until smooth. Serve chilled with cold meats.

CHERRY TOMATO SALSA

2 ctns. cherry tomatoes, cut in quarters
1 clove garlic, pressed
1 T. red onion, diced
1 T. sugar
1-1/2 T wine vinegar
2 T. jalapeños, seeded and diced
2 T. lime juice

Combine all ingredients except sugar. Slowly sprinkle half the sugar and taste. Add remaining if desired. Should be slightly sweet tasting.

CHERYL'S FRESH SALSA

10 fresh tomatoes, diced
4 jalapeños, seeded
6 New Mex long green chiles, roasted (see pg. 29), peeled and seeded

1/2 large onion, chopped
1/8 c. fresh cilantro
1 clove garlic, minced
salt and pepper to taste

Combine tomatoes, onion, garlic and cilantro. Add salt and pepper. Dice chiles and jalapeños and add to bowl. Stir and chill.

CHERYL'S EXTRA SPECIAL QUESO

1 2 lb. box Velveeta
1 c. taco sauce
salt, pepper and garlic
   powder to taste

1 c. diced green chiles
   roasted, peeled and
   seeded

Dice cheese and put in a large microwave bowl. Add the rest of the ingredients to bowl. Cover and microwave for 2 minutes, stir. Microwave and stir every 2 minutes until cheese is melted. Milk can be added to dilute if it is too thick. Serve with chips or on top of burgers.

CHILE RADISH SALSA

1 serrano pepper
2 jalapeño peppers
1 Anaheim (or long green New Mexico pepper)
(All above peppers roasted, peeled, seeded and finely chopped, (see pg. 29)
1 large clove garlic
1 c. radishes, finely chopped
1 c. cucumber, seeded and finely diced
5 scallions, finely chopped
2 c. tomatoes, finely diced and drained
3 T. fresh lime juice
3 T. olive oil
1/2 c. cilantro, chopped
salt to taste

(continued)
Combine all ingredients in a bowl and refrigerate 1 hour. Drain off excess liquid before serving.

CHILEAN SALSA

2 T. olive oil
1 T. red wine vinegar
1/3 c. water
4 fresh jalapeños, seeded
    and minced

2 cloves garlic, minced
1/2 c. onion, minced
1/2 c. cilantro, minced
1 tsp. oregano, minced
salt to taste

Combine oil, vinegar and water in a bowl and whisk until combined. Add remaining ingredients and let stand 2 hours to blend. Can be stored in refrigerator up to 1 week. This is hot!

COLORFUL SALSA

- 3 tomatoes, diced
- 2 jalapeños, seeded and diced
- 1/2 ea. red, yellow and green bell pepper chopped
- 1 T. sugar
- 1 T. olive oil
- 1 T. wine vinegar
- 1 T. fresh cilantro, chopped
- 1 T. fresh parsley, chopped

Combine all ingredients and serve warm or chilled.

CHARRED CORN AND CHILE SALSA

2 med. ears of corn
1 small tomato seeded and finely chopped
1 med. Anaheim chile, seeded and finely chopped
2 cloves garlic, minced
2 T. lime juice
1 T. ground, dried chile
salt to taste

Remove and discard husks and silk from corn. Place on highly oiled grill 4 to 6 inches from medium coals. Cook, turning as needed until kernels are browned (about 8 minutes).

Meanwhile in a large bowl combine tomato, chile, garlic, juice and ground chile. Cut kernels from cobs and stir into tomato mixture. Season to taste. If made ahead, let cool then cover and chill for up to 4 hours. Serve at room temperature.

FESTIVE CORN SALSA

5 jalapeño peppers, seeded and chopped
1 small bell pepper, diced
1 medium tomato, diced
1 T. lime juice
1/2 c. fresh corn
1 small red onion, chopped
1 clove garlic, minced
3 T. olive oil
1 T. fresh basil, chopped

Combine all ingredients and allow to stand at room temperature before serving. Goes well with grilled meats and chicken.

MEXICAN CORN SALSA

3 T. olive oil
3 T. flour
1/4 c. bell pepper, chopped
1/2 c. green chiles, diced

1/4 tsp. dry mustard
1-1/2 c. tomato juice
2 c. corn, removed from cob, blanched and cooled

Heat oil and stir in flour and whisk until smooth. Add bell pepper, chiles, mustard, and tomato juice and simmer until thickened slightly. Remove from heat and add corn.

ROASTED CORN SALSA

- 1/2 c. red onion, finely chopped
- 1/4 c. Anaheim pepper, roasted (see pg. 29) and seeded
- 1 tsp. vegetable oil
- 4 c. fresh corn, blanched and cooled
- 1 red bell pepper, diced
- 1/4 c. lime juice
- salt to taste

Combine corn, bell pepper and remaining ingredients in a bowl and stir well. Refrigerate before serving. Serve with beef or pasta.

EASY SALSA

1 ctn. sour cream
1 pkg. spaghetti sauce
   seasoning mix
4 oz. green chiles, diced
parsley

Combine well and chill overnight. Sprinkle with parsley before serving. Good as condiment with beef.

FREEZER SALSA

5 lbs. tomatoes, peeled and chopped
1 green bell pepper, seeded and diced
1/2 c. jalapeños, diced
1 c. dark brown sugar
1 c. cider vinegar
1 T. cinnamon
1 tsp. cumin
1/2 c. onion, diced

Simmer tomatoes, both peppers, and onion for 1 hour. Add remaining ingredients and simmer 30 minutes more. Cool and puree in blender. Freeze in containers, thaw and reheat in the microwave oven.

FRIJOLE SALSA (Bean)

1 can (10-1/2 oz.) frijoles drained
4 T. onion, minced
2 T. olive oil
1 clove garlic, pressed
1 jalapeño, diced
1/4 c. wine or water

Combine frijoles and onions and sauté lightly in oil. Remove from heat and cool slightly. Add remaining ingredients. This salsa is excellent with beef.

GARDEN HERB SALSA

- 1-1/2 c. plum tomatoes, diced
- 1/2 c. ea. red and yellow bell pepper, diced
- 1/4 c. green onion, minced
- 1 T. jalapeño, seeded and minced
- 1 T. fresh tarragon, chopped
- salt to taste
- 2 T. balsamic vinegar
- 2 cloves garlic, crushed
- 1/4 c. cilantro, chopped

Combine all ingredients in a bowl and mix well. Refrigerate at least 30 minutes. Great with fish and fun in burritos.

GARLIC SALSA

2/3 c. olive oil
4 cloves garlic, pressed
2 T. lime juice

2 T. lemon juice
1 tsp. oregano
1 tsp. dried cilantro

Combine all ingredients and mix well. Serve at once. This is an excellent addition for meats and fish and can be used with flavored pasta.

GREEN CHILE SALSA

8 New Mexico green chiles, roasted, (see pg. 29) peeled, seeded and diced
2 plum tomatoes, blackened and chopped
1 tsp. oregano
1 tsp. cilantro, chopped
1/2 tsp. marjoram
1 T. cider vinegar
1 T. olive oil

Combine all ingredients. Serve with enchiladas, seafood, and chicken.

HOT STUFF SALSA

2 onions, chopped
3 cloves garlic, minced
2 T. olive oil
3-1/2 c. ripe, crushed tomatoes
1 c. jalapeños. seeded and chopped
1 T. cumin
1 tsp. salt

Sauté onions and garlic in olive oil. Add tomatoes and chile and simmer until thick. Add cumin and salt to taste. Cool and serve.

ITALIAN SALSA

8 plum tomatoes, diced   1 tsp. garlic, minced
3 T. red onion, finely diced   3 T. olive oil
3/4 c. basil leaves, julienne   1 tsp. salt

Combine all ingredients and allow to stand at room temperature for 1 hour.

You can add 1 T. of balsamic vinegar for a spicier flavor. Good with pasta, fish, or chicken.

MEAT SALSA

1/2 c. jalapeños, seeded and diced
2 T. allspice
1 tsp. nutmeg
1 tsp. cinnamon
1/4 c. lime juice

Combine all ingredients together. Use over grilled or baked meat. Spoon over meat last few minutes of cooking.

JALAPEÑO SALSA

1 T. olive oil
3/4 c. jalapeños, seeded and chopped
2 cloves garlic, minced
1/4 c. onion, chopped
salt to taste

3 c. tomatoes, peeled, seeded and chopped
1 T. red wine vinegar
1 T. cilantro, chopped
1 T. green olives, chopped

Sauté jalapeños, garlic and onion until onion is soft, 3-5
(more)

minutes. Add tomatoes and cook until they are soft. Add the remaining ingredients and cook a few minutes longer to blend flavors. Add salt. Let salsa stand for at least 30 minutes. Stir well before serving.

You can make a milder salsa by using fewer jalapeños and adding green bell peppers.

MUSHROOM BACON SALSA

1 T. smoked bacon
1/2 lb. portabella
   mushrooms, sliced
1 T. cilantro
1 jalapeño pepper
1/8 tsp. salt
1 T. finely chopped onion

Sauté bacon in a skillet over medium heat until cooked through, about 5 minutes. Add sliced mushrooms and raise heat to medium high and sauté, stirring often until mushrooms are soft and slightly brown, about 6 minutes. Transfer to a bowl and add remaining ingredients.

(continued)
Will keep refrigerated a day or two but is best if eaten right away. Serve hot or at room temperature. Serve with chips, in a salad or on steak or chops. Makes about 1 cup.

MUSHROOM & TOMATO SALSA

- 1 portabello mushroom
- 3 T. olive oil
- 1/2 c. onion, diced
- 3 plum tomatoes, blackened
- 1 c. sun dried tomatoes in oil, diced
- 3 T. red bell pepper, minced
- 2 T. garlic
- 1-1/2 T. fresh parsley, minced
- 2 tsp. balsamic vinegar
- 2 T. lemon juice
- salt and pepper to taste

Brush mushroom with a little olive oil and grill until
(more)

(continued)

tender. Dice and transfer to a bowl. Sauté the onion for 5 minutes over medium heat. Add to mushrooms. Cut the blackened tomatoes in half and squeeze out the seeds and juice. Chop and add to the bowl. Add remaining T. olive oil and remaining ingredients and mix well. Good with pasta.

NEW MEXICAN SALSA

1/2 red onion, minced
1/2 tsp. garlic powder
1/4 c. cilantro, chopped
1 T. cider vinegar

3-5 jalapeños, seeded
5 med. tomatoes, peeled
salt to taste
1/2 c. tomato sauce

Put all ingredients except sauce in food processor or blender. Chop and then stir in tomato sauce. Add salt to taste. Chill at least 1/2 hour before serving. NOTE: Heat level increases with time. Refrigerate or freeze for future use.

OLIVE SALSA

- 4 med. tomatoes, chopped
- 1 4 oz. can black olives, drained
- 6 green onions, chopped
- 1 fresh Anaheim chile, roasted (see pg. 29), seeded and diced
- 1 T. lime juice
- 3 T. fresh cilantro, chopped
- 1/2 tsp. chile powder
- 1/4 tsp. cumin

Combine all ingredients and chill 24 hours.

BLACK OLIVE SALSA

3 lbs. Roma tomatoes, chopped
1-1/2 c. black olives, sliced
1/4 c. red onion, diced
1/2 c. fresh cilantro, chopped
1 T. white wine vinegar

Combine all ingredients and chill for at least one hour before serving.

BLACK OLIVE AND CHIVE SALSA

1 c. plum tomatoes, diced
1/4 c. fresh chives, chopped
1/4 c. Kalamata olives, pitted and chopped
1/8 tsp. pepper
1-1/2 tsp. Dijon mustard
2 cloves garlic, crushed

Combine all ingredients and mix well. Refrigerate at least 30 minutes. Good with almost any meat.

RIPE OLIVE AND CHARRED ONION SALSA

- 3 med. sweet onions, skin on, halved
- 1/4 c. olive oil
- 1/4 c. balsamic vinegar
- 1 T. white wine vinegar
- 1 tsp. red pepper flakes
- 1 c. whole, pitted ripe olives
- 2 tsp. oregano

Place onion halves, cut side down in a shallow pan. Bake in a 425°degree oven for 30 minutes or until onions are slightly soft and cut sides are blackened.

(more)

When cool enough to handle, discard skins and trim stems. Put onions in food processor or blender with oil, vinegars and red pepper flakes. Process in 2 or 3 second bursts or just until coarsely chopped. Add olives and oregano and process 2 to 4 seconds until just chopped.

TWO OLIVE SALSA

1 lg. onion, cut into 8 wedges
2 T. olive oil
1 tsp. sugar
2 c. tomatoes, seeded and chopped
1/3 c. green olives, pitted and chopped
1/3 c. Greek olives, pitted and chopped
3 T. fresh basil, chopped
1 T. capers, drained
2 tsp. red wine vinegar
1 tsp. anchovy paste

Preheat oven to 450°. Place onion wedges on baking

sheet and brush with olive oil and sugar. Season with salt and pepper. Roast until golden brown, turning occasionally, about 30 minutes. Combine remaining ingredients in large bowl. Chop roasted onion and combine with remaining 1 T. olive oil and stir into tomato mixture. Season to taste.

CARROTS AND BLACK OLIVE SALSA

2 c. carrots, finely grated
10 Kalamata olives, pitted
   and minced
1/4 c. olive oil

2 T. fresh lemon juice
1-1/2 tsp. lemon zest
cayenne powder to taste
salt to taste

Combine all ingredients. Serve with chicken or fish.

PICO DE GALLO

1 lg. onion, chopped
3-4 cloves garlic, chopped
3 med. tomatoes, chopped
1 tsp. sugar
4 jalapeños, seeded and chopped
2 T. fresh cilantro
salt to taste

Mix all ingredients together and refrigerate. Will keep for several days.

TEXAS PICO DE GALLO

2 c. tomatoes, diced
1/2 c. onion, finely diced
2 T. jalapeño chiles, minced
salt to taste
1/4 c. cilantro, minced
2 T. lime juice
1/2 tsp. garlic salt

Combine all ingredients and mix well. Chill before serving.

QUICK SALSA

1 lb. tomatoes, peeled, seeded and drained	1/2 c. green chiles, seeded and chopped
1/4 c. chopped onion	1/4 tsp. sugar
1 clove garlic, minced	1 tsp. vinegar
salt to taste	Tabasco sauce to taste

Combine all ingredients in blender or food processor. Process briefly so vegetables are still chunky. Adjust seasonings. Let stand at room temperature for at least 30 minutes.

RED'S SALSA

1 ea. large yellow and red
    bell pepper, chopped
5 jalapeño peppers, seeded
1/3 c. white onion
salt and pepper to taste

1 T. cilantro
3-1/2 c. whole peeled
    tomatoes
1-1/2 c. green chiles,
    roasted, peeled and
    seeded

Put peppers and onion into food processor or blender
(more)

and process for about 10 seconds. Add salt and pepper. In a separate bowl, mix the tomatoes, cilantro and green chiles. Then add to food processor and blend for 5 seconds more.

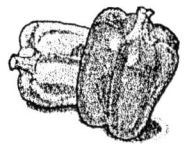

SALSA CRUDA (Tomato and Green Chile Sauce)

6 med. tomatoes, peeled and finely chopped
1/2 c. green chiles, roasted (see pg. 29), peeled and seeded
1/2 c. minced onion
1 tsp. salt
Jalapeños, seeded, to taste

Mix tomatoes with green chiles, onion, salt and jalapeños to taste. (About 1 jalapeño to each cup of sauce will make it HOT!)

(more)

This sauce can be served as a side dish with a meal, or added to any meat or vegetable dish. It can be as hot as you like simply by adding more jalapeños. Makes about 3 cups.

SALSA CILANTRO

1 8 oz. sour cream
1/2 c. mayonnaise
1 c. fresh cilantro, finely minced

1/4 tsp. onion salt
1/2 c. green chiles, diced
1 jar (3 oz.) pimentos, diced

Blend all ingredients and chill. Great with chicken or fish.

SALSA PICANTE

1 bell pepper, any color, seeded and diced
1 med. red onion, chopped
2 small jalapeños, seeded and diced
2 stalks celery, cut into 3" lengths
1 8 oz. can tomato sauce

Cook all ingredients together, simmering for 15 minutes. Add water to cover the vegetables, if necessary. Cool and place in blender or food processor and blend until smooth. Can be reheated and used as a sauce for fish or chicken.

SALSA VERDE

1/2 c. red onion, chopped
2 cloves garlic, pressed
2 T. olive oil
1-1/2 c. water

1/2 tsp. cumin
6 Anaheim chiles, roasted (see pg. 29), seeded and and diced

Sauté onion and garlic in oil until onion is soft. Add cumin, water and chiles and simmer for 20 minutes.

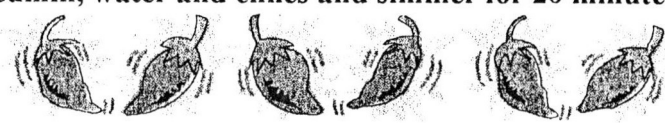

SALSA VINO

1-1/2 c. white wine
3 T. sugar

1/2 c. dried mint leaves
1/2 c. dried cilantro

Mix wine and sugar and boil gently over medium heat until sugar is dissolved. Let cool and stir in mint and cilantro. Let stand for at least 1 hour to blend flavors. Great with beef or lamb.

SUMMER VEGETABLE SALSA

4 tomatoes, diced
1 zucchini, uncooked and diced
1 yellow squash, uncooked and diced
2 jalapeño chiles, diced
2 T. olive oil
2 T. lime juice
1/3 c. fresh cilantro
1 sm. jar diced pimentos, drained

Combine all ingredients and mix well. Refrigerate overnight. Serve as a relish.

TEQUILA SALSA

1/2 c. olive oil
1/2 c. lime juice
1/2 c. tequila
2 T. Triple Sec
1/2 c. diced green chiles

Combine all ingredients. If using as a salsa, chill. Can be used as a marinade for chicken or turkey.

THAI SALSA

3 c. cucumbers, seeded, peeled and chopped
1 c. green onion, chopped
3/4 c. radishes, chopped
1/4 c. fresh ginger, minced
1/4 c. fresh mint, chopped

3 T. fresh lime juice
2 T. sugar
1 T. minced garlic
1-1/2 tsp. sesame chile oil

Combine all ingredients in a large bowl and season with salt. Cover and refrigerate about 1 hour. Stir before serving.

TOMATILLO SALSA I

- 1 small onion, finely chopped
- 2 cloves garlic, minced
- 1/2 c. fresh jalapeños, chopped
- 2 T. fresh cilantro, chopped
- 1 13 oz. can tomatillos, drained (fresh can be substituted)
- Pinch of sugar

Combine ingredients and adjust seasonings. Allow to stand at least 30 minutes. Stir well before serving.

Moderately hot, great with chips, burritos, as a topping for meat or chicken.

TOMATILLO SALSA II

3/4 c. tomatillos, husked and diced (about 8)
1/4 c. red bell pepper, diced
1/4 c. red onion, diced
2 T. orange juice
3 T. white wine vinegar
2 T. fresh lime juice
2 T. fresh lemon juice
1 T. sugar
1/2 tsp. jalapeño, seeded and minced

Puree 1/4 c. tomatillos in food processor or blender.

(more)

VERSATILE SALSA

3 c. tomatoes, diced
3 c. Anaheim peppers, roasted (see pg. 29), seeded and diced fine
1 c. cider vinegar
1 c. cilantro, diced

Combine and cook for 1 hour over medium heat. Remove from heat and let cool. Stir in cilantro.

YELLOW SALSA

- 2 c. tomatoes, diced
- 1 8-1/4 oz. can pineapple chunks, drained
- 1 c. papaya, peeled and diced
- 1 jalapeño, seeded and diced
- 2 T. lime juice

Mix all ingredients and let stand covered in refrigerator for several hours. A delicate flavor for fish or chicken.

FRUIT & DESSERT SALSAS

FRUIT & DESSERT SALSAS

Apricot Salsa	**117-118**
Banana Salsa	**119**
Roasted Banana Salsa	**120**
Cherry Mango Salsa	**121-122**
Butterscotch Salsa	**123**
Chocolate Salsa	**124**
Chocolate Pistachio Mint Salsa	**125**
Cranberry Salsa I	**126**
Cranberry Salsa II	**127-128**
Fig Pistachio Salsa	**129**

Honey Salsa	130
Island Salsa	131
Lime Salsa	132
Mango Salsa	133
Quick Mango Salsa	134
Cucumber, Bell Pepper & Mango Salsa	135
Melon Salsa	136
Orange Peach Salsa	137
Papaya Salsa	138
Another Papaya Salsa	139
Habañero Papaya Salsa	140
Peach Salsa	141

Pear Ginger Salsa	142
Pear Black Olive Salsa	143-144
Pecan Salsa	145
Pineapple Salsa I	146
Pineapple Salsa II	147
Pineapple Salsa III	148
Pineapple Avocado Salsa	149
Pineapple Mango & Cucumber Salsa	150
Raspberry Salsa	151
Rum Raisin Salsa	152
Strawberry Salsa	153
Strawberry Balsamic Salsa	154

Summer Fruit Salsa	155-156
Watermelon Salsa	157

APRICOT SALSA

1/2 red bell pepper, roasted (see pg. 29) and chopped
olive oil
1 small onion, chopped
1 small tomato, chopped
1 jallapeño pepper, minced
2 apricots, chopped
2 T. dark rum
apple cider

Sauté onion in olive oil until soft. Add tomato and jalapeño and sauté another 5 minutes. Add apricots and cider to cover and boil down until cider is almost
(more)

(continued)
boiled off. Add roasted bell pepper and stir. Add run
and flambe. Serve hot over fish or chicken.

BANANA SALSA

2 bananas
1/4 c. sugar
1/2 c. cream

1 tsp. vanilla
1 T. rum

Mash bananas and add remaining ingredients and mix well. Serve over cake or ice cream.

ROASTED BANANA SALSA

4 ripe bananas
1 tsp. dark rum
1 tsp. vanilla

1 tsp. maple syrup
1/2 tsp. brown sugar
12 pecans, finely chopped

Preheat oven to 350°. Put bananas, in their skins, on a cookie sheet and roast for 30 minutes. (Their skins will turn dark brown.) Let cool, peel, dice and place in a bowl. Add remaining ingredients and fold together. Good with chicken or pork.

CHERRY MANGO SALSA

1 onion, chopped
1 clove garlic, minced
2 jalapeños, seeded and
 minced
Juice of 2 limes
1 jar mango, diced

juice of 1 lg. lemon
2 T. white wine or cider
 vinegar
1 lb. fresh cherries, seeded
 and halved

Heat olive oil in a skilled and add onions, peppers and garlic. Sauté over medium heat until onions get limp,
(more)

about 5 to 8 minutes. Add lime juice and vinegar. Bring to a boil, add cherries and mango. Simmer for 8 to 10 minutes, stirring occasionally. Remove from heat and chill. This can be served warm as well.

If a smooth sauce is preferred, puree in food processor or blender before chilling. Great on chicken or fish.

BUTTERSCOTCH SALSA

1/2 c. sugar	3 T. butter
1/2 c. brown sugar	2/3 c. cream
1 c. corn syrup	2 tsp. vanilla

Mix all ingredients and bring to a boil, simmer gently for 5 minutes. Remove from heat and stir in vanilla. Cool and refrigerate. Perfect over ice cream.

CHOCOLATE SALSA

1/2 c. cocoa
1 c. milk
1 c. sugar
1 tsp. cornstarch

1 c. cream
1 T. butter
1 T. any flavor liqueur

Stir cocoa, milk, sugar, cornstarch and cream together in pan and cook over medium heat until thickened. Remove from heat and add liqueur and butter.

CHOCOLATE PISTACHIO MINT SALSA

1/2 c. Swiss or Mexican chocolate
1/2 c. unsalted pistachio nuts, chopped and toasted
1 med. ripe banana
1 tsp. fresh mint, minced

In a bowl, gently mix together all ingredients. This is best if used quickly. Great on ice cream or used in cookie dough.

CRANBERRY SALSA I

1 lb. bag fresh cranberries
1 lg. red apple
1 lg. orange, rind included
2 c. sugar
2 jalapeños, seeded and diced

Seed apple and orange and cut into chunks. Rinse cranberries. Place in food processor or blender and chop together. Stir in sugar and jalapeño. Mix well. Prepare at least 48 hours before serving. This salsa improves with age and freezes well. Good for gifts.

CRANBERRY SALSA II

1 12 oz. pkg. cranberries
2 whole oranges
1/2 c. sugar
1 bunch cilantro
1/2 med. red onion
2 jalapeños, seeded
chunk fresh ginger, peeled
1/4-1/2 tsp. chile powder

Put cranberries and juice from one orange and quartered orange in food processor or blender. Peel other orange and add it in sections. Add sugar and cilantro and process or 1-2 minutes, keeping texture.

(more)

Slice the onion and jalapeños and add, also ginger root and process. Add chile powder to taste, blend.

This keeps very well and can be made ahead of time. The heat increases as it stands, so beware!

FIG PISTACHIO SALSA

1 c. dried figs, diced (use fresh in season)	1 tsp. freshly grated orange zest
1/4 c. boiling water	1 T. honey
2 T. fresh lemon juice	1/4 unsalted pistachio nuts, chopped

Toss figs in a bowl with boiling water until plump (eliminate water if using fresh figs). Add remaining ingredients and mix well. Keeps for a few days. Serve over ice cream or pound cake.

HONEY SALSA

4 T. vegetable oil
4 T. lime juice
2 T. honey
1 T. fresh cilantro, chopped

3 lg. tomatoes, diced
1 jalapeño or serrano chile seeded and minced

Blend all ingredients and mix well. This is very popular in southwest Texas as a condiment to grilled chicken.

ISLAND SALSA

1 c. pineapple, peeled and chopped
1 c. mango, peeled and chopped
1 c. red bell pepper, chopped
2/3 c. kiwi fruit, peeled and chopped
1/2 c. red onion, diced
1/4 c. fresh cilantro, finely chopped
1 tsp. fresh lime juice
1 tsp. serrano chile with seeds, minced
ground white pepper

Combine all ingredients in bowl, season with white pepper and salt to taste. Chill.

LIME SALSA

1 lg. ripe tomato, finely diced
8 med. tomatillos, husked, rinsed and chopped
1/4 c. yellow or red bell pepper, minced
2 T. red onion, minced
1 tsp. grated lime peel
1 T. lime juice

Combine all ingredients. Cover and chill up to 4 hours.

MANGO SALSA

1 serrano chile, roasted (see pg. 29), seeded and minced
1 mango, peeled, seeded and diced
2 T. mango pulp
1 slice white onion, diced
1 clove garlic, minced
1 T. cilantro, minced
1/2 c. red bell pepper, diced

In a bowl, mix all ingredients together and chill.

QUICK MANGO SALSA

2 lg. firm, ripe mangos
1/2 c. scallions, finely chopped
1/2 c. coriander, minced
1/4 c. fresh lime juice
pepper to taste
Tabasco or other hot sauce to taste

Cut the mangos into thick sections, cutting as close to the pits as possible. Trim off skin and dice the flesh. Do this over a dish to catch juice. Put mangos and juice in a bowl and fold in remaining ingredients. Refrigerate until ready to serve. Excellent with fish or chicken.

CUCUMBER, BELL PEPPER & MANGO SALSA

3 c. mango, chopped
1 c. cucumber, seeded and diced
1 med. red onion, diced
1 med. red bell pepper, seeded and finely diced
1 small tomato, finely diced
3-4 jalapeños, seeded and finely diced
3 T. lime juice
1 T. cilantro, chopped
1/2 tsp. red pepper flakes
1/2 tsp. ground cumin
1 tsp. ginger, grated

Mix all ingredients and refrigerate at least 1 hour before serving. Serve with blue corn chips or as a relish for chicken or fish.

MELON SALSA

3/4 c. honeydew melon, diced
3/4 c. cantaloupe, diced
3/4 c. watermelon, diced
1-1/2 tsp. sugar
1 T. fresh lime juice
1-1/2 tsp. serrano chile, seeded and minced
1-1/2 tsp. fresh mint, minced

Combine all ingredients. Good as a side dish with chicken or fish.

ORANGE PEACH SALSA

1 c. peach preserves 3 T. Grand Marnier
1/4 c. orange juice

Heat preserves and juice, stirring constantly until preserves are melted. Cool slightly and stir in Grand Marnier. Can be used as a seasoning for baked ham or pork.

PAPAYA SALSA

- 2 papayas, semi ripe, diced
- 1/2 red onion, chopped
- 2 cloves garlic, finely diced
- 2 T. ginger root, finely diced
- juice of 1 lime with pulp
- fresh basil l leaves, julienne
- dash Tabasco sauce, to taste
- cumin, to taste
- salt and pepper
- 2 T. vegetable oil

Mix all ingredients together and chill. Can be used as a salsa or as a topping for fish or chicken.

ANOTHER PAPAYA SALSA

1 medium papaya, peeled, seeded and chopped	1/4 c. cilantro, snipped
1 medium cucumber, seeded and chopped	1/4 c. vegetable oil
	1/4 c. vinegar
1/2 c. onion, chopped	2 packets sweetener
	salt and pepper to taste

Combine papaya, cucumber, onion and cilantro. In a small jar, combine oil, vinegar, sweetener, salt and pepper. Shake well to mix. Pour over papaya mixture and toss to coat. Cover and chill.

HABAÑERO PAPAYA SALSA

1 ripe papaya
2 limes
10 habañeros, seeds removed
1 T. garlic, chopped
2 T. honey
1 tsp. ginger, chopped
1/2 c. vinegar

Dice peppers, juice limes and put in blender or food processor. Blend until smooth. Place in a saucepan and simmer for 10 minutes, cool and refrigerate.

To make this salsa less hot use fewer habañeros. Great with chicken and pork.

PEACH SALSA

1 can (15 oz.) peaches, drained and diced or fresh
1/4 c. green onions, diced
1 T. lemon juice
1 bell pepper, any color, diced
2 tsp. mint leaves, chopped
1 c. green chiles, diced
1/4 tsp. ground ginger

Mix well and refrigerate overnight. This salsa freezes well.

(continued)

onion and cilantro and mix well. Crush the cumin seed and add to the vinegar mixture with salt. Stir then pour mixture over fruit and mix gently. Cover and refrigerate at least 1 hour. Don't make this salsa too far ahead of time as the fruit will get soft.

WATERMELON SALSA

2 c. watermelon, seeded and coarsely chopped
2 T. onion, chopped
2 T. water chestnuts, chopped
2-4 T. Anaheim peppers, seeded
2 T. balsamic vinegar
1/4 tsp. garlic salt

Combine all ingredients and mix well. Refrigerate at least 1 hour.

MISCELLANEOUS

MISCELLANEOUS

Anchovy Spread	160
Chile Butter	161
Creamy Salsa for Omelets	162
Garlic Lemon Butter	163
Mexican Coffee	164
Mexican Hot Chocolate	165
Salsa for Spinach Salad	166
Salsa Sandwich Spread	167-168
Sassy Salsa Spread	169
Texas Jalapeño Mayonnaise	170
Vegetable Salsa Marinade	171

ANCHOVY SPREAD

6 anchovy fillets, mashed
1 clove garlic, pressed
1-1/2 T. jalapeños, 1 seeded and diced
1/2 c. olive oil
3 T. parsley, fresh or dried
lemon juice to taste
8 oz. cream cheese, softened

Add garlic to mashed anchovies, add chiles, oil, parsley and lemon juice. Combine with softened cream cheese and mix completely.

CHILE BUTTER

1/2 c. diced green chiles
1 lb. butter, softened
garlic powder

1/4 c. fresh cilantro, chopped
1 tsp. lime juice

Blend all ingredients well. This butter has many uses and keeps well in the refrigerator. Wonderful with scrambled eggs and on rolls and crackers. If frozen, use dried cilantro.

CREAMY SALSA FOR OMELETS

4 T. butter or margarine
4 T. flour
1-1/2 c. milk or light cream
1/2 c. onion, diced
1 c. green chiles, diced
1 3 oz. jar pimentos, diced
1 tsp. dried cilantro

Melt butter and stir in flour. Whisk until flour is absorbed. Gradually stir in milk or cream and stir until thickened. Add remaining ingredients. Serve hot over omelets.

GARLIC LEMON BUTTER

1 c. butter, softened
1 clove garlic, crushed
1 tsp. seasoned salt
1 tsp. seasoned pepper

1 tsp. grated lemon peel
2 T. fresh lemon juice
1 T. red pepper sauce

Cream butter adding garlic, salt and pepper. Blend thoroughly. Add remaining ingredients and mix well.

MEXICAN COFFEE

4 c. water   1/2 c. instant coffee
1/3 c. dark brown sugar   4 cinnamon sticks

Combine water and sugar and bring to a boil, stirring until sugar is dissolved. Reduce heat and stir in coffee, simmer 2 minutes. Pour into individual mugs and add a cinnamon stick.

MEXICAN HOT COCOA

1/4 c. cocoa
1/4 c. sugar
3/4 tsp. cinnamon

1 qt. milk
1/3 c. heavy cream
1 tsp. vanilla

Combine cocoa, sugar and cinnamon. Set aside. Heat 1 c. milk until bubbly, stir in cocoa mix and whisk until smooth. Gradually stir in remaining milk so a slow boil continues. Remove from heat and add cream and vanilla. Mix well.

SALSA FOR SPINACH SALAD

1/2 c. olive oil
2 cloves garlic, crushed
2 T. garlic wine vinegar
1 c. green chiles, diced
1/2 c. crisp bacon, diced
1 tsp. dried cilantro

Combine all ingredients. Just before serving, warm 10 seconds on full power in microwave oven.

SASSY SALSA SPREAD

4 oz. sharp Cheddar cheese, shredded	1/2 c. pitted ripe olives, chopped
1 pkg. (8 oz.) cream cheese softened	2 green onions, thinly sliced
1 c. thick & chunky salsa, divided	1/4 c. fresh cilantro, chopped and divided
	1/3 c. red bell pepper, chopped

Combine Cheddar cheese, cream cheese and 1/2 salsa

(more)

and mix well. Stir in bell pepper, olives, green onions and 2 T. cilantro. Spread cheese mixture into bowl, smoothing top and spoon remaining salsa evenly over top. Garnish with remaining cilantro.

Serve with a variety of crudites: vegetables, small slices of baguette, crackers.

SALSA SANDWICH SPREAD

2 pkgs. (3 oz.) cream cheese with chives
1 pkg. (3 oz.) cream cheese with pimento
1 c. diced green chiles

Soften cream cheese, stir in chiles. Spread over sliced ham or tortillas and roll up. Serve chilled.

TEXAS JALAPEÑO MAYONNAISE

1-3/4 c. mayonnaise
2 T. water
2 T. white vinegar
pepper to taste

1 jalapeño chile, seeded
1 garlic clove
1/2 c. fresh cilantro

In food processor or blended combine all ingredients and blend until smooth. Salt to taste.

VEGETABLE SALSA MARINADE

2/3 c. red wine vinegar
1 c. vegetable oil
1 tsp. dried sweet basil

1 T. lime juice
dash Tabasco sauce

Combine and mix well. Marinade vegetables at least 2 hours or until well chilled. Use yellow and green squash (uncooked) and mushrooms with this.

NEED GIFTS?

Are you up a stump for some nice gifts for some nice people in your life? Here's a list of some great cookbooks. Just check 'em off, stick a check in an envelope with these pages, and we'll get your books off to you. Add $2.75 for shipping and handling for the first book and then $.50 cents more for each additional one. If you order over $50.00, forget the shipping and handling.

Mini Cookbooks
(Only 3 1/2 x 5) With Maxi Good Eatin' - 160 or 176 pages - $5.95

- ❏ Alabama Cooking
- ❏ Arizona Cooking
- ❏ Arkansas Cooking
- ❏ Dakota Cooking
- ❏ Dixie Cooking
- ❏ Georgia Cooking
- ❏ Illinois Cooking
- ❏ Indiana Cooking
- ❏ Iowa Cookin'
- ❏ Kansas Cookin'
- ❏ Kentucky Cookin'
- ❏ Michigan Cooking
- ❏ Minnesota Cookin'
- ❏ Missouri Cookin'
- ❏ New Jersey Cooking
- ❏ New Mexico Cooking
- ❏ New York Cooking
- ❏ North Carolina Cooking
- ❏ Ohio Cooking
- ❏ Pennsylvania Cooking
- ❏ South Carolina Cooking
- ❏ Tennessee Cooking
- ❏ Virginia Cooking
- ❏ Wisconsin Cooking
- ❏ Amish-Mennonite Apple Cookbook
- ❏ Amish-Mennonite Berry Cookbook
- ❏ Amish-Mennonite Peach Cookbook
- ❏ Amish-Mennonite Pumpkin Cookbook
- ❏ Amish & Mennonite Strawberry Cookbook
- ❏ Apples! Apples! Apples!
- ❏ Apples Galore
- ❏ Basil A-Z
- ❏ Berries! Berries! Berries!
- ❏ Berries Galore!
- ❏ Bountiful Blueberries
- ❏ Cherries! Cherries! Cherries!
- ❏ Cherries Galore
- ❏ Citrus! Citrus! Citrus!
- ❏ Cooking Seafood & Poultry with Wine
- ❏ Cooking with Asparagus
- ❏ Cooking with Cider
- ❏ Cooking with Fresh Herbs
- ❏ Cooking with Garlic
- ❏ Cooking with Spirits
- ❏ Cooking with Sweet Onions
- ❏ Cooking with Wine
- ❏ Cooking with Things Go Baa
- ❏ Cooking with Things Go Cluck
- ❏ Cooking with Things Go Moo
- ❏ Cooking with Things Go Oink
- ❏ Cooking with Things Go Splash
- ❏ CSA Cookbook (**$4.95**)
- ❏ Crazy for Basil
- ❏ Crockpot Cookbook
- ❏ Dixie Cookbook
- ❏ Good Cookin' From the Plain People
- ❏ How to Make Salsa
- ❏ Kid Cookin'
- ❏ Kid Fun
- ❏ Kid Money

- Kid Pumpkin Fun Book
- Midwest Small Town Cookin'
- Muffins Cookbook (Veggies, Fruit, Nut)
- Nuts! Nuts! Nuts!
- Off To College Cookbook
- Peaches! Peaches! Peaches!
- Pecans! Pecans! Pecans!
- Pumpkins! Pumpkins! Pumpkins!
- Recipes for Appetizers & Beverages Using Wine
- Recipes for Desserts Using Wine
- Some Like It Hot
- Soup's On!
- Southwest Cooking
- Super Simple Cookin'
- To Take the *Gamey* out of the Game Cookbook
- Wild Rice Cookbook
- Working Girl Cookbook

Larger Mini Cookbooks
176 - 204 pages - $6.95

- Cooking with Mulling Spices
- Grass-Fed Beef Recipes
- The Grilling & BBQ Cookbook
- Holiday & Get-Together Cookbook
- Veggie Talk Coloring & Story Book

- Winter Squash Cookbook
- The Zero Calorie Chocolate Cookbook

In-Between Cookbooks
(5 1/2 x 8 1/2) - 150 pages - $9.95

- Adaptable Apple Cookbook
- Amish Ladies Cookbook - Old Husbands
- Amish Ladies Cookbook - Young Husbands
- Amish Ladies Carry-To-The-Field Cookbook
- Amish Ladies It's-Time-To-Rest-The-Horses Snacks
- Amish Ladies Plump-'Em-Up-A-Little-Bit Cookbook
- An Apple A Day Cookbook
- Baseball Moms' Cookbook
- Basketball Moms' Cookbook
- Bird Up! Pheasant Cookbook
- Buffalo Cookbook
- Camp Cookin'
- Catfish Cookin' Cookbook
- Civil War Cookin', Stories, 'n Such
- Cookin' Panfish Cookbook
- Cooking Ala Nude

(continued)

- Cooking for a Crowd
- Cooking Up Some Winners Cookbook
- Cooking with Beer
- Cooking with Moonshine
- Country Cooking
    Recipes from my Amish Heritage
- Cow Puncher's Cookbook
- Das Hausbarn Cookbook
- Eating Ohio
- Farmers Market Cookbook
- Feast of Moons Indian Cookbook
- Football Mom's
- Funky Duck Cookbook
- Halloween Fun Book
- Herbal Cookery
- Hunting in the Nude Cookbook
- Ice Cream Cookbook
- Indian Cooking Cookbook
- Japanese Cooking
- Keep The Skinny Kid Skinny Cookbook
- Kids' No-Cook Cookbook
- Mad About Garlic
- Make the Play All-Sport Cookbook
- Mormon Trail Cookbook
- New Cooks' Cookbook

($9.95 continued)

- ❏ No-Stove, No-Sharp Knife Kids' Cookbook
- ❏ Outdoor Cooking for Outdoor Men
- ❏ Plantation Cookin' Cookbook
- ❏ Pumpkin Patch, Proverbs & Pies
- ❏ Shhh Cookbook
- ❏ Soccer Mom's Cookbook
- ❏ Southwest Ghost Town Cookbook
- ❏ Southwest Native American Cookbook
- ❏ Southwest Vegetarian Cookbook
- ❏ Trailer Trash Cookbook
- ❏ Turn of the Century Cooking
- ❏ Vegan Vegetarian Cookbook
- ❏ Venison Cookbook
- ❏ Western Frontier Cookbook

Biggie Cookbooks
(5 1/2 x 8 1/2) - 200 plus pages - $11.95

- ❏ Aphrodisiac Cooking
- ❏ Barn Raising & Threshers Cookbook
- ❏ Bride's Guide (1910) to the Culinary Arts Cookbook
- ❏ Buy Fresh, Buy Local
- ❏ Covered Bridges Cookbook
- ❏ Depression Times Cookbook
- ❏ Dial-a-Dream Cookbook
- ❏ Discover the Phillipines Cookbook
- ❏ Flat Out, Dirt Cheap Cookin'
- ❏ Grandma's Cookbook
- ❏ Grits Shall Rise Again
- ❏ Have You Considered Cooking
- ❏ Hormone Helper Cookbook

($11.95 continued)

- ❏ I-Got-Funner-Things-To Do Cookbook
- ❏ Le Ricette (Italian) Cookbook
- ❏ Little "Ol Blue Haired Church Lady Cookbook
- ❏ Lumber Camp & Saw Milling Cookbook
- ❏ Mississippi River Cookbook
- ❏ Quilters' Cookbook
- ❏ Real Men Cook on Sunday Cookbook
- ❏ Southern Homemade Cooking
- ❏ Spice 'N Wine Cookbook
- ❏ Taste of Las Vegas Cookbook
- ❏ Vegetarian Wild Game Cookbook
- ❏ Victorian Sunday Dinners
- ❏ Wild Critter Cookbook

HEARTS 'N TUMMIES COOKBOOK CO.
3544 Blakslee St. • Wever, Iowa 52658
1-800-571-2665

Name _____

Address _____

_____ Ph.# _____

*You Iowa folks gotta kick in another 6% for Sales Tax.

Pour into a medium bowl and mix in remaining tomatillos and the other ingredients. Cover and refrigerate at least 30 minutes. This can be prepared one day ahead.

TOMATILLO TOMATO SALSA

3 med. tomatoes, chopped
6 tomatillos, husks removed and chopped
1 jalapeño, seeded and diced
1 T. lime juice
6 green onions, cut in 1/2" pcs.
1/2 bunch cilantro, minced

Combine all ingredients and chill.

PEAR GINGER SALSA

1-1/2 c. pears, diced
1/3 c. red bell pepper, diced
1/3 c. golden raisins
2 green onions, thinly sliced
1 jalapeño, seeded and minced
1 T. white wine vinegar
2 tsp. minced ginger
salt to taste

Combine all ingredients and mix well. Cover and refrigerate overnight. Will keep up to 3 days in the refrigerator. Makes 2 cups.

PEAR BLACK OLIVE SALSA

1 T. vegetable oil
3 pears, peeled, cored and diced
1 tsp. sugar
8 Kalamata olives, pitted and sliced
1 T. apple cider vinegar
3 plum tomatoes, roasted and diced
1 small poblano chile, roasted, peeled, seeded and diced
1 small red bell pepper, seeded and diced

Heat oil in skillet and sauté the pear with sugar over
(more)

(continued)
medium low heat for 2 minutes. Transfer to bowl and add remaining ingredients. Combine thoroughly.

PECAN SALSA

1-1/2 c. water
1 c. light brown sugar
1 c. sugar
3 T. lime juice

2 c. whipping cream, unwhipped
1/2 c. green chiles, diced
2 c. pecans, chopped

Heat water and add both sugars and stir until dissolved. Raise heat and boil gently 5 minutes. Remove from heat and slowly stir in cream. Add remaining ingredients, stirring well. Can be used as a gravy, good over chicken.

PINEAPPLE SALSA I

2 c. fresh pineapple, diced
1 c. red bell pepper, diced
1/2 c. fresh cilantro, chopped
1/4 c. red onion, diced
1 clove garlic, crushed
2 T. jalapeño pepper, seeded and minced
1 T. white wine vinegar
1 T. olive oil
pepper to taste

Combine all ingredients and refrigerate 30 minutes before serving. Put on top of grilled fish, chicken or pork.

PINEAPPLE SALSA II

2 c. fresh pineapple, diced   4 tsp. fresh cilantro, minced
2 T. red bell pepper, minced 1 tsp. sugar
2 tsp. serrano chile, seeded 1 T. rice wine vinegar
   and minced

Combine all ingredients and let stand 1 hour to meld flavors.

PINEAPPLE SALSA III

2 c. tomatoes, drained and chopped
1 sm. can crushed pineapple, drained
1 jalapeño, seeds removed and diced
1 T. lime juice
4 T. fresh cilantro, chopped
2 T. red onion, minced

Combine all ingredients and refrigerate uncovered until well chilled. Great with fish.

PINEAPPLE AVOCADO SALSA

1 c. fresh pineapple, diced
2 plum tomatoes, seeded and diced
1 firm ripe avocado, diced
1/2 c. sweet onion, diced
1/4 c. fresh cilantro, diced
1-1/2 tsp. jalapeño chile, seeded and diced
3 T. fresh lime juice
3 T. fresh orange juice
2 T. olive oil

Combine all ingredients and season with salt to taste.

PINEAPPLE MANGO & CUCUMBER SALSA

1/2 c. pineapple, diced small
1/2 c. firm ripe mango, diced
1/2 c. cucumber, peeled and diced
1/3 c. red bell pepper, diced
1/3 c. tomato, diced
3 T. green onion or chives chopped fine
3 T. cilantro, chopped
jalapeño, diced to taste
salt to taste

Mix all ingredients together and adjust seasoning. Chill to marinate and blend flavors. Good with fish or chicken.

RASPBERRY SALSA

2 c. raspberries, fresh or frozen
3 T. sugar
1 T. cornstarch, dissolved in 2 T. water
3 T. raspberry liqueur

Heat raspberries and sugar to boiling. Add cornstarch mixture and stir well. Remove from heat and stir in liqueur. Wonderful on ice cream.

RUM RAISIN SALSA

1 c. raisins
2 c. sugar
2 tsp. cornstarch
2 tsp. lemon juice

3 T. butter or margarine
1/2 c. pecans, chopped
1/2 c. dark rum

Simmer raisins in 1-1/2 c. water about 30 minutes. Stir in sugar and cornstarch, simmer 5 more minutes. Remove from heat, stir in butter. When melted, stir in lemon juice, pecans and rum. Cover and refrigerate.

STRAWBERRY SALSA

1 lb. strawberries, fresh or frozen
1/2 c. sugar
1/2 c. cream
1/2 c. orange flavored liqueur

Place all ingredients in blender and mix on medium speed. Serve over ice cream.

STRAWBERRY BALSAMIC SALSA

1 pint strawberries, stemmed and sliced
4 tsp. balsamic vinegar
1 T. red wine
1 tsp. sugar
1/4 tsp. black pepper

Combine all ingredients. Great as a summer dessert with whipping cream.

SUMMER FRUIT SALSA

3 T. raspberry vinegar
1 T. brown sugar
1 c. mango, cantaloupe or peach, chopped
1 ripe kiwi, peeled and chopped
1/2 c. strawberries, chopped (1 papaya can be used)
1/4 c. green onions, diced
1 T. fresh cilantro, chopped
1 tsp. cumin seed
salt to taste

In small bowl combine vinegar and brown sugar and blend well. In a larger bowl, combine the fruit, green

(more)